THE STORY OF

ROBERTO CLEMENTE, ALL-STAR HERO

BY JIM O'CONNOR

ILLUSTRATED BY STEPHEN MARCHESI

A YEARLING BOOK

ABOUT THIS BOOK

The events described in this book are true. They have been carefully researched and excerpted from authentic autobiographies, writings, and commentaries. No part of this biography has been fictionalized. To learn more about Roberto Clemente, ask your librarian to recommend other fine books you might read.

Thanks and appreciation to Bill Bell and John Bell, who are great Roberto Clemente fans

Published by
Dell Publishing
a division of
Bantam Doubleday Dell Publishing Group, Inc.
1540 Broadway
New York, New York 10036

ISBN: 0-440-40425-8

Published by arrangement with Parachute Press, Inc.
Printed in the United States of America
March 1991
10 9 8 7 6 5 4 3
OPM

Contents

Prologue

Three Rivers Stadium, Pittsburgh, Pa.
September 30, 1972

Roberto Clemente, the superstar of the Pittsburgh Pirates, crouched at home plate. All of his attention was focused on New York Mets pitcher Jon Matlack. Clemente was waiting, bat ready, for Matlack's pitch.

Roberto Clemente was a man with a mission. He was one of baseball's greatest hitters, and this was a very important moment for him. His next hit would be number 3,000 of his career in professional baseball. Only ten players had ever reached that magic number. Roberto was determined to become number eleven.

All season long, Jon Matlack had kept Roberto from getting a hit whenever they faced each other. Today, more than ever, Matlack wanted to keep Roberto hitless. He did not want

1

to be the pitcher who gave up such an historic hit.

Just the day before, in a game against the Mets, Roberto had almost succeeded in getting number 3,000 off of Mets pitcher Tom Seaver. He hit a weak grounder up the middle, but the official scorer ruled it an error. He said that Roberto would have been out if Mets second baseman Ken Boswell hadn't bobbled the ball. Some Pittsburgh fans and players disagreed with the official scorer. They felt it was a clean hit.

But the official scorer's word was law.

At first Roberto had been upset. For years he had felt cheated out of hits, batting titles, and Most Valuable Player awards. He was convinced that because he was both Puerto Rican and black he did not receive the recognition he deserved as one of the best players in baseball. He felt he continually had to prove himself. Now, once again, he felt robbed.

After thinking it over, however, Roberto changed his mind. "Deep down," he said after the game, "I would rather have a clean hit."

Now Roberto had another chance. On the mound Matlack started his windup. Clemente narrowed his eyes. His body tensed as Matlack pitched a curve ball. Roberto was ready. His bat slashed through the air and connected solidly with the ball, sending it sailing deep into left-center field.

Roberto had just gotten hit number 3000!

Over thirteen thousand Pittsburgh fans jumped to their feet screaming as Roberto raced around first base and ran to second. It was a double!

When Roberto reached second base he tipped his hat to the fans. The fans' roar grew even louder. Then umpire Doug Harvey walked over to second base and handed the ball to Roberto to keep. A few moments later Roberto Clemente left the game to a standing ovation. The game wasn't over yet, but he was tired and sore from a season's worth of injuries.

Pittsburgh was leading in the National League East. They would soon play the Cincinnati Reds, the top team in the National League West, for the National League pennant. Roberto wanted to rest his aching body before the playoffs started.

Roberto was looking forward to the playoffs. If the Pirates could beat the Reds, they had a good chance of winning their second consecutive World Series.

He was doubly happy because he had just completed another outstanding season. At age thirty-eight, when many professional baseball players were over the hill, Roberto seemed to be a stronger player than ever. Who knew how many more seasons he could play?

No one at Three Rivers Stadium that day knew that they had witnessed Roberto Clemente's last regular season at bat. Roberto himself didn't know it.

There was no way anyone could know that in just thirteen weeks tragedy would strike. A plane crash would end Roberto Clemente's life—and one of the most amazing careers in baseball.

Born to Play Baseball

Roberto Walker Clemente was born on August 18, 1934, in Carolina, Puerto Rico. Carolina was a poor farming community just outside of Puerto Rico's capital, San Juan.

Roberto was one of seven children. He was the youngest boy. His father, Melchor Clemente, worked in the fields of a sugar cane plantation. It was backbreaking work under a hot sun, and Melchor was not paid very well. Even when he was promoted to foreman and his pay doubled, he made only four dollars a week.

Luisa, Roberto's mother, also worked. She got up each day at 1 A.M. to do laundry for the owner of the sugar cane plantation. Then she went home to look after her husband and Roberto and his brothers and sisters.

Melchor was a "jibaro"—a descendant of the mountain people of Puerto Rico. Jibaros are known to be proud and hard-working.

5

Their families are very important to them. Jibaros believe in caring for others who are less fortunate than themselves. As Melchor's son, Roberto was also a jibaro. Throughout his life he would display the dignity and warmth typical of his people.

From his parents Roberto learned the value of hard work. Melchor and Luisa taught him that no person was better than anyone else simply because he or she has more money or lighter skin.

Roberto learned these lessons well. As a baseball player and in his personal life, he always stood up for what he thought was right. Some people didn't like this. They called Roberto arrogant and pushy. But that did not stop him from speaking his mind.

Although Roberto never felt poor when he was growing up, there was never extra money in the Clemente household. Once, to earn money for a secondhand bicycle, Roberto got a job. Every morning he carried a heavy milk can half a mile from the store to a neighbor's house. He earned a penny a day. It took him years to save up the twenty-seven dollars he needed for the bike!

Looking back, Roberto said it did not seem like a big thing. "At six o'clock every morning I went for the milk. I wanted to do it. I wanted to have work."

But there was something Roberto wanted even more than work. He wanted to play baseball.

"Roberto was born to play baseball," Luisa told reporters years later, when her son had already become a Major League star. "I can remember when he was five years old. He used to buy rubber balls every time he had a chance. He played in his room, throwing the ball against the wall and trying to catch it. There were times when he was so much in love with baseball that he didn't even care for food."

Roberto would squeeze the rubber balls to develop his hand and arm muscles. When there was no money for a real ball he would make one out of old magazines. Sometimes he and his friends would play baseball with old tin cans and tree branches.

Roberto lived for baseball. The local field was muddy and studded with trees, but Roberto didn't mind. He would play there all day, game after game.

Luisa wasn't completely happy with her youngest son's passion for baseball. Roberto was a quiet, shy student who got good grades. Luisa wanted her son to become an engineer so that he could escape from the sugar cane fields of Carolina. She could not imagine that baseball would lead to a better life for him.

When Roberto was fourteen his mother made a desperate attempt to turn him into an engineering student. She tried to burn his baseball bat! But Roberto saw the bat in the fire and pulled it out before it was ruined. Finally, Luisa gave up and let him play baseball.

"I wanted to become a ball player," Roberto later said. "And the more I thought about it, the more I became convinced God wanted me to. I was sure I came into the world for this reason."

At night Roberto would lie on his bed and listen to the games of a Puerto Rican baseball team, the San Juan Senators, on his radio. One of the Senators' stars was a black left fielder named Monte Irvin.

Irvin became Roberto's first idol. Monte Irvin was a good hitter *and* a good thrower.

Monte Irvin had starred in the Negro Leagues in the days before professional baseball was integrated. Sometimes Roberto would take a bus ride into San Juan to see the Senators play. Afterward he would wait outside the locker room until Monte Irvin left. But he was always too shy to speak to his hero.

In 1947 another Negro League player, Jackie Robinson, was signed by the Brooklyn Dodgers. Robinson became the first black man to play in the Majors in modern times. Irvin was rated an even stronger player than Robinson. Soon after Robinson joined the Dodgers, Irvin was signed by the New York Giants.

By the time Roberto was in high school he was playing baseball in three different leagues. He played regular baseball for his high school, making the all-star team three years in a row. The all-star team was made up of the best players from several different high school teams. Roberto also played in the San Juan youth baseball league. And when he was fourteen he discovered softball, too.

In reality Roberto didn't discover softball—it discovered him!

One day a man named Roberto Marin saw Roberto Clemente playing a game of baseball with tin cans and an old broomstick. Marin was a salesman for the Sello Rojo rice company, and he also coached his company's softball team. He watched in amazement as Roberto hit the cans time after time. He immediately convinced Roberto to play for the Sello Rojo softball team.

Roberto played shortstop. He thrilled the fans with his diving, acrobatic plays. But he also experienced some difficulties on the team. For some reason Roberto had a tough time getting hits. Many of Sello Rojo's games were played at night under lights. His coach thought that Roberto was having trouble following the pitches. But Marin wasn't worried. He knew that Roberto Clemente had great talent. The hitting would come.

After a while Marin decided that Clemente was too slow to play shortstop, so the young player was moved to the outfield. There, he began learning the skills that would make him the best defensive right fielder in baseball.

Although Roberto spent most of his free time playing baseball, he also found time to join the high school track team. He could jump over six feet in the high jump, and he could throw a javelin 195 feet. He was seriously considered for the 1952 Puerto Rican Olympic team!

But Marin had other plans for Roberto Clemente. He had never seen another player with as much raw talent as Roberto. Marin was convinced that Roberto would someday play professional baseball.

One day Marin had some exciting news for Roberto. Al Campanis, the number one scout for the Brooklyn Dodgers, was traveling throughout the Caribbean searching for new talent. The Dodgers were one of the most awesome professional baseball teams in the United States. There was going to be an open tryout for the team the following day in Santurce, a suburb of San Juan.

"You're going," Marin told Roberto.

Campanis did not have high hopes of finding anyone for the Dodgers that day. Open tryouts were usually a waste of time. Only once in a very long while did he find a really good player.

Seventy-two kids showed up for the tryouts that day. Campanis lined the boys up in the outfield and had them each throw to home plate. Throw after throw fell short or far off target. Campanis was about to give up when a throw came in straight and hard. It hit the catcher's mitt with a loud pop.

"Uno más," Campanis yelled in Spanish to Roberto Clemente. "One more!"

The next throw was as good as the first.

"I couldn't believe my eyes," Campanis recalled years later. "This kid throws a bullet. On the fly."

Campanis quickly told the other seventy-one boys to go home. Only Roberto stayed for the rest of the tryout.

When Campanis had Roberto run the sixty-yard dash he was shocked again. Roberto ran the dash in a sizzling 6.4 seconds in sneakers and long pants. The world record, held by trained track stars who ran in special track shoes and shorts, was 6.1 seconds. Campanis asked Roberto to run the dash again. Another 6.4!

Next they moved to the batting cage. For twenty minutes Roberto hit one line drive after another. Meanwhile, Campanis noticed that Roberto was standing far away from the plate. Campanis told his pitcher to start throwing the ball outside and away, where it would be hard for Roberto to hit. He wanted to see what Roberto would do. Roberto still hit the ball.

"Shots. He hit shots all over the place. The kid swings with both feet off the ground and hits line drives to right and sharp ground balls up the middle.

"How could I miss him? He was the greatest natural athlete I have ever seen as a free agent."

Campanis and the Dodgers wanted to sign Roberto. But one thing stood between Roberto and his first Major League contract: his age. Roberto was just seventeen and going to high school. He had to be eighteen before he would be allowed to play in the Major Leagues.

Still, Roberto was ready to start a real baseball career. Three days later a local semi-pro team, the Santurce Crabbers, offered him a contract. Pete Zorilla, the owner of the Crabbers, had seen Roberto play in a game and told him, "You can play for me right now."

The Puerto Rican teams did not have to follow the same rules for signing young players that the big-league teams did. The Crabbers offered Roberto $500 as a signing bonus. In 1952 that was an incredible amount of money for a Puerto Rican farm boy. When Zorilla saw the tattered mitt that Roberto used he also promised Roberto a new glove if he would sign.

Roberto took the contract to his father. After talking it over with his son, Roberto Marin, and Pete Zorilla, Melchor agreed that Roberto could play for the Crabbers. Roberto signed the contract.

Roberto was so excited! The Crabbers played in the Puerto Rican Winter League. Many of the teams in the Winter League had professional ball players from the Major Leagues in the U.S. They came to Puerto Rico to enjoy the warm weather and to stay in shape. Playing with Major Leaguers would be a real challenge for Roberto. The competition could be tough for a seventeen-year-old boy who was still in high school.

The Crabbers' manager was James "Buck" Clarkson. In addition to managing the team Buck played shortstop. After watching Roberto hit, field, and throw, Buck told him he would play right field and bat first in the lineup.

But Roberto did not play much. Pete Zorilla did not believe in putting young ball players up against the Major Leaguers too often. He felt that star pitchers like Satchel Paige, who had dominated the Negro Leagues and the Puerto Rican Winter League for years, could easily destroy a young hitter's confidence.

Roberto was very unhappy. He had never

been "sat down" before. That winter Roberto came to bat only seventy-seven times in seventy games. The rest of the time he sat on the bench.

Buck Clarkson tried his best to encourage Roberto. "I told him he'd be as good as Willie Mays some day," said Clarkson. "And he was."

Even though he was disappointed, Roberto always appreciated Clarkson's help. "Clarkson helped me as much as anyone," Roberto remembered later. "I was just a kid, but he insisted the older players let me take batting practice."

Santurce won the Winter League championship that year. That meant the team would travel to the neighboring island of Cuba to compete for the Caribbean title. Roberto was very excited. Except for a few road games with the Crabbers, he'd never been away from Carolina. But his spirits sank when Zorilla decided to leave Roberto behind. He wanted to take more experienced players instead.

Robert was crushed. His pride was wounded. No one believed in Roberto more than he believed in himself. He couldn't understand Pete Zorilla's reason for leaving him behind.

Perhaps that was when Roberto's determination to prove himself began. Many times during his career Roberto would feel that people did not appreciate him or treat him fairly. Each time he would drive himself to even greater success and prove the other people wrong.

In February of 1954 the Brooklyn Dodgers came back to Roberto with the contract that Al Campanis had promised in 1952. In the summer of 1954 Roberto would be nineteen and eligible to play in the Major Leagues. The Dodgers offered Roberto a $10,000 bonus and a salary of $5,000. Roberto received another offer, too. The Milwaukee Braves wanted Roberto to play with them. They offered him $35,000. This was a major bonus in 1954. The average ball player made less than $20,000 a season.

But money was not the most important thing to Roberto. He was a Dodgers fan. Besides, he knew some of the Dodgers from the Puerto Rican League. On February 19, 1954, he signed the Dodgers contract.

Roberto's career as a Major League baseball player was about to begin.

Montreal

When Roberto Clemente signed with the Dodgers their outfield was already hard-hitting and strong-armed. Right fielder Carl Furillo had led the National League the previous season with a .344 average. (A batting average is determined by dividing the number of hits in a season by the number of official at-bats, or turns batting.) Duke Snider, the center fielder, had hit .336, including forty-two home runs. Jackie Robinson—who had made baseball history seven years earlier when he became the first black man to play modern professional baseball—played left field, with an average of .329.

The last thing the '54 Dodgers needed was another outfielder! Roberto soon discovered that being signed by a team and actually playing for it were two very different things. He was a nineteen-year-old Puerto Rican who knew no English, and there was no room for him in the Dodgers outfield. When spring training ended Roberto did not join the Dodgers in Brooklyn. Instead, he was sent to play with the Montreal Royals, a Dodgers farm club. Farm clubs are Minor League teams that prepare young players for the Major League teams.

In the past, other talented Dodgers players had been sent to play with the Royals. Jackie Robinson had played his first year of pro baseball in Montreal. He loved the city and the people who accepted a black player right away.

Roberto was not as happy. The cool weather, French language, and food were strange to him. He was homesick for Puerto Rico. The only thing he liked about Montreal was the fans. They knew baseball, and they quickly let Roberto know that they appreciated his fiery style of play—when he played.

Unfortunately, Roberto didn't get to play very often. This was because the Brooklyn Dodgers were hiding him.

Usually a younger player is sent to a farm club so that he can play every day and gain

experience. While he plays he is evaluated by his coaches and also by scouts from competing baseball teams.

Today, a player who does well in a farm club can go on to play for the Major League team that signed him. Or he can be traded to another team by the club that owns his contract for a more experienced player. Or he can be "drafted," or signed, by another club at the end of the year.

In 1954 a Minor League player being paid more than $4000 for the season could be drafted by another club at the end of the year. Because Roberto had signed with the Dodgers for $5000, he was up for grabs.

The Dodgers knew that if Roberto played a lot, other teams would realize what a talented player he was. Their only hope was to keep Roberto out of sight so he would not attract the attention of another club.

So instead of playing, Roberto sat on the Montreal bench getting angry. In one early season game he blasted a home run more than 400 feet over the left field wall of Delerimier Stadium, where the Royals played. But the next day he was back on the bench. Later that season, Roberto hit three triples in one game. He sat out the next game. In another game, when it was Roberto's turn to hit, the bases were loaded. Rather than let him go to bat, the manager replaced Roberto with a pinch hitter.

All in all, Roberto got to play in only eighty-seven games out of 152. His batting average was only .257, and he had just twelve runs batted in, or RBIs. An RBI is a run scored by another player as a result of a player's batted ball.

Despite Roberto's poor statistics, other teams were after him. Milwaukee was still interested in having Roberto play for them. So were the New York Giants. They already had one sensational outfielder, Willie Mays. With Roberto, the Giants' outfield would be even more spectacular.

A third team, the Pittsburgh Pirates, was also keeping an eye on Roberto. Branch Rickey, the general manager of the Pirates, was a keen judge of baseball talent. In fact, he and his main scout, Clyde Sukeforth, had brought Jackie Robinson to the Major Leagues in 1947. Rickey and Sukeforth had been with the Dodgers when they discovered Jackie Robinson. Now they were working for the Pirates. Together they made another great find.

Sukeforth never forgot the first time he saw Roberto Clemente play, at a Royals game in Richmond, Virginia. Sukeforth was "scouting" Joe Black, a Montreal pitcher.

"I arrived just in time for the pre-game workouts. I saw Clemente throwing from the outfield, and I couldn't take my eyes off him. Later in the game he was used as a pinch hitter, and I liked his swing. I started asking questions and learned he was a bonus player and would be eligible for the draft."

Sukeforth called Branch Rickey and told him about the promising young right fielder. Rickey sent another Pittsburgh scout, Howie Haak, to check out Roberto.

Haak told the Montreal Royals' manager, Max Macon, that he was evaluating Roberto Clemente. Macon was desperate to save Roberto for the Dodgers. He played Roberto even less so that Haak wouldn't be able to see Roberto in action. Haak got to watch him play in just one game in two weeks.

Roberto had no idea why he was playing even less than before, but it made him angry.

He went to Campanis, the scout who had first offered him the contract with the Dodgers, and asked what was going on. Campanis told him not to worry. That did not satisfy Roberto.

Finally, Roberto had had enough. In a game against the Rochester Red Wings, Roberto was again replaced with a pinch hitter in the first inning. He was so angry that he stormed back to his hotel and began packing his suitcase. He was going to leave the Royals and go home.

If Roberto left, it would put an end to Howie Haak's plans for him. Haak knew that Roberto had to play the entire Minor League season or the Pirates would not be able to draft him. If he quit now the Dodgers would have him for at least another season.

Haak left Red Wings Stadium and caught up with Roberto at the hotel. He begged Roberto not to leave.

"Finish the year, and next season you'll be playing every day with the Pirates."

Roberto did not know Haak, but he believed him. He unpacked his suitcase and finished the season with Montreal.

Meanwhile, the Pittsburgh Pirates suffered

through a humiliating season. They finished dead last.

For Branch Rickey, there was at least one big consolation. As the last-place team, the Pirates were guaranteed first pick in the draft.

They would take Roberto Clemente.

A Rookie in Pittsburgh

When the long season with Montreal finally ended Roberto returned home to Puerto Rico. Once again he was eating his mother's cooking, speaking Spanish with his family and friends, and relaxing in the warm sun. The Pittsburgh Pirates hadn't officially drafted him yet, but he knew that his days in the Dodgers organization were almost over. Meanwhile, he could play Winter League ball with the Santurce Crabbers.

That year the Crabbers were probably the strongest team ever to play in Puerto Rico. Pitchers Reuben Gomez and Sam Jones won thirteen and fourteen games respectively. The team's owner had signed several Major Leaguers, including Don Zimmer, Willie Kirkland, George Crowe, and Willie Mays. Mays had just won the 1954 National League batting title with a .345 average.

Willie Mays and Roberto quickly became close friends. With four years of big-league experience under his belt, Willie became Roberto's teacher.

Playing beside Willie in the outfield, Roberto studied everything he did. And when they were sitting on the bench waiting to bat, Willie would coach Roberto on hitting.

"Don't let the pitchers here show you up," Willie would tell him. "Get mean when you go to bat. If they try to knock you down, act like it doesn't bother you. Get up and hit the ball. Show them."

Roberto learned his lessons well. By the end of the winter season, Willie led the league with a .395 average. Roberto was fourth with an average of .344. The Crabbers finished first in the Winter League.

Representatives from the Major League teams were also busy that winter. Officials from all the Major League clubs met in Florida for the annual winter baseball meetings. During the meetings they discussed rule changes and made trades. They also held the "draft." That was where each team picked available players—

players who weren't bound to a team by contract.

In 1955 Branch Rickey, the Pittsburgh Pirates' general manager, decided to stop by Puerto Rico before going to Florida. Since they had finished in last place in the National League, the Pirates would have first pick in the draft. Rickey had already heard a lot of good reports about Roberto Clemente. Now he wanted to get a good look at Roberto for himself before the draft.

Rickey watched the Crabbers play several games. He thought Roberto looked very good on the field.

"I like the way you play," Rickey said to Roberto when they finally met. "Can you do the same things in the Major Leagues?"

Roberto's answer surprised Rickey. Most young players would simply have said yes. Some would have been too tongue-tied to answer at all. Not Roberto.

"I don't know," he told Rickey. "I've never seen a Major League game. I don't know if the players in my country are better than the ones in the Major Leagues."

Branch Rickey had just seen Roberto play in the same outfield as Willie Mays, one of the best players in baseball. He knew one thing: Roberto was already Willie's equal. That was good enough for Rickey and the Pittsburgh Pirates. They chose Roberto in the draft.

The team Roberto joined in 1955 did not have a lot going for it. The Pittsburgh Pirates had lost at least a hundred games each season for three seasons in a row. Almost every year, they finished last in the National League.

In one respect the Pirates were the perfect club for Roberto. With Pittsburgh he would have time to learn the ins and outs of the Major Leagues. He would get plenty of opportunity to play, without the kind of pressure players of a first-division team were under. If he had stayed with the Dodgers, the pressure to play outstanding baseball immediately would have been much greater.

When Roberto left Puerto Rico that spring he didn't even know where Pittsburgh was. But he got off to a great start with the Pirates. He had an inside-the-park home run against the New York Giants. In the ninth game of the season he drove in the run that gave the Pirates their first win that season.

But Roberto had a lot to learn. Forbes Field, where the Pirates played, was bigger than other fields he had played on. Even though he was a powerful hitter, Roberto found that it was hard to hit home runs at Forbes Field. He later explained how he had to adjust his hitting. "When I first saw Forbes Field I said, 'Forget home runs.' I was strong, but nobody was that strong. I became a line drive hitter."

His new method worked. By mid-May Roberto had a very strong .360 average.

Playing right field at Forbes presented another challenge. The right field wall angled out to a very deep center field, which meant that Roberto had a lot of ground to cover. To make matters worse, the wall was covered with ivy! Balls that hit the wall bounced off in all sorts of crazy directions. Sometimes balls would bounce up into the ivy and not come out at all! Then the unlucky right fielder would have to search for the ball while the runner took an extra base or two.

During practice Roberto set out to learn

the secrets of the wall. He had teammates hit line drives off the wall until he could anticipate where any ball would go. Once Roberto had the ball in his glove, the strong throwing arm that had impressed Dodgers scout Al Campanis took over. In the Pirates' first fifty games, Roberto's powerful throws helped his teammates make ten outs.

Even though Roberto was playing well, he wasn't happy off the field. He was lonely, and he didn't have any close friends on the team. Some of the other players made fun of his accent.

Roberto was only twenty years old, and he still spoke almost no English. "Not to speak the language . . . that was a terrible problem," Roberto said later. "Not to speak the language meant you were different."

Pittsburgh was not integrated in 1955. Most of the black people lived in one area, which was called "the Hill." When Roberto went to Forbes Field he wouldn't see another black except for two teammates. Sometimes he would stay for hours after games signing autographs because he had nothing else to do and couldn't face going back to the lonely hotel room where he lived.

Roberto could not get used to the racial prejudice he encountered in Pittsburgh. It started in spring training when a Pittsburgh sportswriter labeled Roberto a "Puerto Rican hot dog." Sometimes when he played, players from the other team would try to distract him by calling him names.

Although Roberto knew very little English, he knew what the word *nigger* meant. Roberto had been warned that he would experience this kind of verbal abuse. But that didn't make it any easier for him.

"I don't believe in color; I believe in people," Roberto said. "My mother and father taught me never to hate, never to dislike someone because of their color. I didn't even know about that stuff when I got here."

There were two other black players on the Pirates, Curt Roberts and Roman Mejias. They told Roberto that he should keep his mouth shut and live with the abuse.

Roberto just couldn't do that. Throughout his career he would speak up whenever he thought that he or any other player was discriminated against because he was black or Hispanic.

Roberto had other problems, too. His back began bothering him. The winter before he started with the Pirates, Roberto had been in a serious car accident in Puerto Rico. He injured two discs in his back. Now his back still troubled him. Several times the pain was so bad that Roberto asked the team's manager, Fred Haney, to take him out of the lineup.

This started a rumor that stayed with Roberto for the rest of his career. When Roberto said that he couldn't play some of his teammates and the sportswriters didn't believe him. They thought Roberto was just goofing off.

Roberto's teammates knew he had a lot of ability. At 5'11" tall and 185 pounds, Roberto was all muscle. He looked as if nothing could stop him. But his back problems sometimes made playing baseball very difficult.

At that time it was a tradition in baseball for players to "gut it out"—to play no matter what, even when they were injured. Lou Gehrig, who played 2,130 consecutive games, was called "the

Iron Horse." Every manager wanted his players to be like Gehrig. A lot of people didn't think Roberto was living up to this tough image of professional baseball players.

To make matters worse, Roberto went into a hitting slump. Like a lot of rookies—players in their first year on a Major League team—he started trying too hard. Roberto always hated to let a pitch go by without trying to hit it. He swung at nearly every pitch, even bad ones. For every eight times at bat, Roberto struck out once.

Frustrated, Roberto started losing his temper. After striking out, he would return to the dugout and start breaking things, usually batting helmets. Later on he talked about that difficult part of the season: "Once I broke twenty-two helmets. Haney told me it would cost me ten dollars for each one. That's $220 and I didn't make that much money. So I stopped breaking helmets."

By the end of the 1955 season, Roberto's slump had brought his average down to .255. His old team, the Dodgers, won the National League pennant and then the World Series. Once again, the Pirates finished last. The team's manager, Fred Haney, was fired, and Branch Rickey retired as general manager.

It was not the kind of season rookies dream about, but at least it was over. Roberto was determined that he, and the Pirates, would get better.

A Rough Start

Roberto went home to Puerto Rico for the winter. It was so nice to be back home with his family. When he sat in the sun and talked with them Roberto didn't miss Pittsburgh at all.

Roberto had promised the Santurce Crabbers he would play for them in the Winter League that year, but his back was in terrible shape. The pain was so bad that Roberto was able to play in only a few games. At times he didn't think he would be able to play for the Pirates the next year.

Luisa Clemente was still not convinced that baseball was the right career for her son. She kept urging him to go back to school and become an engineer. But Roberto wasn't ready to give up baseball yet.

Playing with the Pirates for one year had given him only a taste of the big leagues. He wanted more. In his heart Roberto knew he could do much better than he had in his rookie year. He was determined to prove that he was a truly outstanding player, not just a "Puerto Rican hot dog" showing off.

"I will try it one more year," he told his mother and father. "If I still hurt, then I will quit."

While Roberto was trying to nurse himself back to health, the Pirates were making trades and trying to strengthen their team. Joe Brown, the new general manager, had made a trade in May that would pay big dividends. He got Bill Virdon, a hard-hitting center fielder, from the St. Louis Cardinals. Virdon, who had been the National League Rookie of the Year in 1955, would play beside Roberto in the outfield for the next nine years.

Next Brown strengthened the Pirates' infield with a promising young Minor Leaguer, second baseman Bill Mazeroski. Like Roberto, Virdon and Mazeroski were excellent fielders and hitters. Roberto was excited that his team now had some real muscle.

The Pirates' new manager was Bobby Bragan. Bragan was a fiery Texan who didn't hesitate to let anyone—players or umpires—know

when he wasn't happy with a play or a call. Like Brown, Bragan was determined to transform the Pirates from losers to winners in one season.

For a while the Pirates looked as if they could go all the way to the World Series. By mid-June they were in first place!

But the team still had some problems. Eventually, their weak pitching and spotty hitting pushed the Pirates lower and lower in the standings.

Still, for Roberto, 1956 was a good year. In late July he turned a triple into an inside-the-park home run against the New York Giants when he ignored Bragan's signal to stop at third base. Roberto's back wasn't bothering him—he missed only seven games all season—and his hitting was strong.

Roberto finished the season with a .311 batting average. He felt confident that 1957 would be an even better year.

But at the start of the 1957 season Roberto's back suddenly went out again. He missed games all season long, and when he did play he had to wear a back brace.

Almost immediately, the press, many fans, and some teammates began accusing Roberto of faking injuries so that he could take it easy.

That kind of talk made Roberto furious. He hated to miss a single at-bat, let alone an entire game. He couldn't understand how anyone could think he would actually *want* to miss any games.

When Roberto's back hurt it threw his whole body out of line. He couldn't swing a bat without pain. His throws from right field lost their speed and accuracy. How could he run when he could barely walk?

Roberto blamed the press for the rumors that surrounded him. He felt that some reporters were out to get him just because he was black and Puerto Rican. He would never forget being labeled a "Puerto Rican hot dog" during his rookie season.

It had been less than ten years since Jackie Robinson had integrated baseball. Some clubs, like the Boston Red Sox, still did not have a black player. Players and fans thought nothing of calling a black player all kinds of names. When Roberto's comments were published some reporters would write what he said in an exaggerated Spanish dialect that made him sound stupid and comical.

Many of the other Latin and black players chose to ignore racist remarks they heard on and off the field. Roberto could not, and would not, do this. "I don't stand for disliking people because of their color," he told his black teammate Curt Roberts. "If that is the case, then I don't want to be living. I am a double nigger . . . for my skin and my heritage."

By early summer the Pirates were doing very poorly in the National League. Manager Bobby Bragan tried everything to get his club to play better, but nothing worked.

Finally, in August, Bragan was fired. The new manager was Danny Murtaugh, a feisty man who once played second base for the Pirates. Murtaugh had a quick temper and a sharp tongue. He didn't hesitate to use both on the umpires, the opposing teams, and his own players.

But his tactics worked. The Pirates played much better with Murtaugh managing them. They won over half of the games that were left in the 1957 season, but it was too late to save it.

The Pirates tied for last place.

That year, Roberto spent the off-season in the Marine Corps Reserves. The many hours of physical exercise and conditioning at Marine boot camp in Parris Island, South Carolina, had a good effect on his ailing back. Suddenly the pain was gone. When he reported for spring training the following season his back was stronger than at any time since his car accident three years earlier.

The new, healthy Roberto Clemente showed everyone what he could do in 1958. At one point the Pirates were in first place. Roberto's batting average was nearly .400. Later in the season, Roberto went into a hitting slump, however, and the Pirates slumped with him. By the time his swing was back on track it was too late for the Pirates to win the National League pennant. But they finished second in the league, behind the Milwaukee Braves.

Pirates fans had high hopes for the 1959 season. If the team could improve on their previous season's record, they might be able to win the National League pennant—for the first time in thirty-two years!

But 1959 turned out to be a heartbreaking year. On May 12 Pirates pitcher Harvey Haddix threw twelve no-hit innings against the Milwaukee Braves, only to lose the game in the thirteenth inning. Five days later Roberto was hit on the right elbow with a pitch. He was unable to play for the next forty days.

While Roberto sat on the bench, Danny Murtaugh got more and more frustrated. He knew that Roberto was key to the Pirates' success. The team was struggling. Murtaugh felt that Roberto was taking too long to recover from his injury. Finally during one game he started yelling at Roberto: "You're faking the injury. Take off the uniform."

"No one takes my uniform while I'm playing for the Pirates," Roberto said. He stayed right where he was.

Roberto finally started playing again in July. The Pirates promptly won seven of their next eight games. Roberto played hard for the rest of the season and ended up with an average of .296. But the Pirates could do no better than fourth place.

The end of the 1959 season marked five years in the big leagues for Roberto. He had a respectable .282 career average. But he had missed almost 140 out of 770 games due to injuries.

Roberto hadn't yet proven himself as the dominant player that Branch Rickey had predicted he would be. But he knew he could do much better. He was only twenty-five years old and was still learning his way around the big leagues.

He knew he could be a great baseball player. And in 1960 Roberto would prove it.

A Year to Remember

1960 was a year the Pirates could do no wrong. All the years of frustration and disappointments were finally wiped out for the Pirates and their fans.

Led by Roberto Clemente, Dick Groat, Bill Mazeroski, Bill Virdon, and Dick Stuart, Pittsburgh snatched first place in May and never let it go.

Now a new cheer was heard in Forbes Field. The Pirates are also called Buccaneers. All year, Pittsburgh fans shouted out, "Beat 'em, Bucs!" And the Bucs didn't let their fans down.

The Pirates specialized in exciting games in which they came from behind in the late innings. They won twenty-three games in their final at-bat.

All year long Roberto's hitting and fielding were spectacular. In May his .353 average propelled the Pirates past the Giants and into first place. Although his bat cooled slightly after that, his average never dropped below .300.

Roberto was great in the field, too. He played right field with an intensity that was sometimes dangerous. He would do anything to get an out.

"In a game at Forbes Field," Roberto's teammate Bill Virdon recalled years later, "he caught the ball over his shoulder and ran into the concrete wall in right field where the fence angled out. He was going headfirst into it. Somehow he threw his head back and got cut under the chin instead of getting hit in the throat. It probably saved his life."

Roberto held up his glove to signal the umpire that he had not dropped the ball. Then he was taken to the hospital to have his chin stitched. Roberto spent the next five games recovering on the bench.

Without Clemente, the Pirates' lead over the second-place team slipped from seven to just two games. As soon as he could, Murtaugh put Roberto back in the lineup.

Late in the season the St. Louis Cardinals suddenly threatened to take over first place. Pittsburgh fans had seen their team choke and blow leads before. Would the Pirates come through for them this time?

On September 25, it all came down to two important games. Pittsburgh was playing the Milwaukee Braves and the Cardinals were playing the Chicago Cubs. The Pirates only needed one—one win over the Braves or one loss by the Cardinals to the Cubs—and the National League pennant would finally belong to them.

When Pittsburgh took the field in Milwaukee the Cardinals and Cubs had already started their game. The Pirates followed the other game in their dugout.

In the fifth inning Roberto was waiting to bat when everyone in the Pirate dugout suddenly burst out with screams and cheers. As Roberto walked to the plate he asked his teammate Dick Stuart, "Did we win it?" Stuart's grin was all the answer Roberto needed. The Cubs had beaten the Cards. The Pirates would go to the World Series!

Roberto promptly smashed a double. Minutes later the Pirates got another hit, and Roberto ran to third base. Ignoring the coach's signal to stop, he raced home. Later, when a reporter asked him why he had not stopped,

Roberto explained, "I wanted to get to the bench and talk about the pennant."

When the Pirates came home from Milwaukee 125,000 fans poured into the streets to celebrate and greet the team.

The Pirates faced a powerful New York Yankees team in the 1960 World Series. Few people expected the Pirates to give the Yankees much of a fight. But after six games, even though the Yankees had outscored the Pirates 46 to 17, the teams were tied at three games each. A team has to win four games to win the World Series.

The seventh and final game of the Series was played in Pittsburgh. After four innings the Pirates led 4–0. The Yankees scored in the fifth and earned four more runs in the sixth inning, to take a 5–4 lead. In the top of the eighth, the Yankees ran the score to 7–4. It looked as if they would win the game—and the World Series.

Then, in the bottom of the eighth, the Pirates staged one of their late-inning rallies and took the lead again, with a score of 9–7. But the Pirate fans couldn't relax for a minute. The next time the Yankees were at bat, they promptly tied the game 9–9!

It was now the bottom of the ninth inning. If the Pirates could score, they would win. Otherwise, the game would go into extra innings. Bill Mazeroski, the Pirates' second baseman, was the first player to bat. Maz smashed the second pitch over the left field wall for a home run!

Fans and players jumped and screamed and hugged each other. "We won! I can't believe it! We won!" That night downtown Pittsburgh became one gigantic party as hundreds of thousands of fans poured into the streets to celebrate.

Walking among them and sharing their joy was Roberto Clemente. Roberto had gotten on base in every game, finishing the Series with a .310 average. But he couldn't just stay in the Pirates' locker room with his teammates. He wanted to be with the fans.

Later, Roberto described what it was like.

"The biggest thrill was when I . . . saw all those thousands of fans in the street. I didn't feel like a player at the time. I've never seen anything like them. We hugged each other. I felt good being with them."

Roberto went home to Puerto Rico a hero.

He stayed with his parents in the new house he had bought for them in Carolina. Although he was tired from the long season and from the excitement and pressure of playing in the World Series, he couldn't relax. He was waiting to hear who had won the National League's Most Valuable Player Award.

Traditionally, the award went to a player on the National League's first-place team. 1960 had been Roberto's best year ever. He had finished with a .314 average, sixteen home runs, and ninety-four RBIs. He had played in all but ten games. Roberto's World Series average was .310.

His fielding had been just as good. Roberto had played right field so well that some people were comparing him to the legendary Mel Ott. A few fans were already saying he could be the best defensive right fielder ever.

Roberto thought he deserved the MVP award in 1960. But he'd heard rumors that his teammate Dick Groat might be chosen by the sportswriters for that honor. Groat had grown up in Pittsburgh and was an excellent short-stop. He'd led the National League in batting with a .325 average. But Groat had only 50

RBIs, and he had missed the entire last month of the season with an injury.

Nevertheless, the baseball writers awarded the MVP to Groat.

Roberto was still in Carolina when he heard the disappointing news. He knew that Groat was a great player and a team leader, but Roberto couldn't help wondering if some of the baseball writers had chosen Groat simply because he was white.

When Roberto saw a list of the players who received votes he exploded. He was only eighth on the list. Not one single writer had given him a first-place vote. Now Roberto was sure that the writers had snubbed him because he was black and Puerto Rican.

When his World Series ring arrived, Roberto put it away instead of wearing it. The ring should have been a symbol of a wonderful season. But to Roberto it was a painful reminder that his outstanding achievements had not been recognized. He still had to prove himself.

Trials and Triumphs

Starting in 1960 Roberto Clemente played season after season of outstanding baseball. His team did not always play as well as he did. But even though the Pirates suffered through some awful seasons, Roberto won the respect and admiration of baseball fans throughout the United States and Latin America.

Roberto was determined to prove that the baseball writers had been wrong not to vote him the Most Valuable Player of 1960. First he went to work on his hitting. He took extra instruction from Pirates batting coach George Sisler. Sisler had won the American League batting title with a .420 average in 1922, and he knew a lot about hitting.

Sisler saw that Roberto was a "natural" hitter who did not need to work on his swing. But Roberto liked to swing at every pitch. Sisler told him to be patient and to "wait on the ball" until he got a pitch he could hit.

Roberto hated to get a base on balls. "You can't walk off the island" was a saying favored by young ball players in Puerto Rico. They believed that the scouts signed only players that got a lot of hits. So Roberto swung at bad pitches as well as good ones. This gave National League pitchers a big edge. Since they knew that Roberto would swing at their "junk," that's what they threw. Roberto struck out on a lot of bad pitches.

Next Sisler had Roberto change to a heavier bat. This helped slow down his swing and gave him added power.

Before long, Sisler and Danny Murtaugh watched in amazement as Roberto began waiting for good pitches. He was hitting hard line drives to every field. Roberto was striking out less and getting more walks. Best of all, he was leading the National League with a .357 batting average.

For the first time Roberto and his manager began to understand and appreciate each other. Although Roberto's many complaints about his aches and pains annoyed Murtaugh, the manager recognized that Roberto was a real competitor who hated to lose.

Each year, the best players from the National League played against the American League's top players in an All-Star Game. Murtaugh was manager of the National League team in the 1961 All-Star Game. Usually the manager plays as many of the All-Stars as possible. This means that most players do not play for the entire game, but are replaced by other "stars." But Murtaugh did not replace Roberto; he left him in for the entire game.

Roberto hit a triple; he knocked in one run with a fly ball; and he drove in the winning run of the game, breaking a tie score in the bottom of the tenth inning.

"He paid me a big compliment," Roberto said after the game. "I don't think I let him down."

When the season ended Roberto was awarded the Silver Bat for the best batting average in the National League, .351. He also won the Gold Glove for the best-fielding right fielder; he had thrown out twenty-seven base runners.

The Pirates did not do as well. They finished sixth in the league.

In 1962 Roberto hit .312 and was voted to the All-Star Team again. But unfortunately his truce with Danny Murtaugh was over. During the season Roberto had had a number of ailments. He complained about a nervous stomach. He also had stitches in his ankle from an accident on the field. He had bone chips in his elbow, and his back always hurt.

Some players suffered silently. Not Roberto. He talked about his health all the time. Sometimes the aches and pains weren't serious, but talking about them made Roberto feel better. Then, when Roberto really was seriously hurt, his teammates and coaches and the sportswriters didn't always believe him.

It was easier for Murtaugh to put up with Roberto's problems when the Pirates were winning. But in 1962 the team couldn't do better than fourth place. Murtaugh's patience was running out.

Twice the manager accused Roberto of not trying hard enough during games. Both times Roberto had serious injuries. He resented Murtaugh for making him play. What really both-

ered Roberto was that Murtaugh didn't believe him. In fact, Roberto felt that Murtaugh and the sportswriters were hard on him just because he was Latin.

"If a Latin or an American Negro is sick," Roberto once said, "they say it is all in his head."

The 1963 season wasn't any easier for Roberto. Although he felt healthy all season long, he still managed to stir up controversy.

In May Roberto was thrown out of a game for striking an umpire after a close call at first base. Roberto claimed he had hit the umpire accidentally as he was trying to get to the dugout. "I just touched his uniform," he said.

Warren Giles, the president of the National League, didn't buy Roberto's explanation. He fined Roberto $250 and suspended him from playing for ten days.

Roberto didn't take the suspension quietly. He complained to the press that the umpires were always unfair to the Pirates. "Every year I lose fifteen or twenty points on close plays at first base. This is the worst year for umpiring." Roberto went on to say that there were "only two or three good umpires" in the entire National League.

Soon afterwards, Roberto went to Puerto Rico to visit his brother Osvaldo, who was dying of cancer. Osvaldo gave him some valuable advice. "He told me to quit fighting the umpires. He said 'You are too good a ball player to worry about them. Just go and play your game.'"

Roberto listened to his brother and stayed out of trouble for the rest of the season. Instead of yelling at the umpires, he would point out the unfair calls against the Pirates to his teammates. The other Pirates thought it was great of Roberto to do this. It was Roberto's first step toward becoming a team leader.

He made the All-Star Team again in 1963, and he finished the year with a strong .320 average. However, Roberto's performance was practically the only bright spot of the Pirates' season. They finished eighth in the league.

That winter, while he was home in Puerto Rico, Roberto made a very important trip to the drugstore. No one knows what ache or pain Roberto was trying to get rid of that January day. But while he was waiting for the druggist, Roberto met a beautiful young girl named Vera Zabala.

Vera was twenty years old. She had also

grown up in Carolina, but she and twenty-nine-year-old Roberto had never met. Roberto asked Vera out on a date, but her parents wouldn't allow their daughter to date someone they didn't know—not even the famous Roberto Clemente.

Finally Vera said she would be allowed to go out with Roberto if four other people came along. For their first date he was going to take her to a baseball game. But it was rained out! Their date must have been a success anyway, because Roberto and Vera continued to date all winter. By the time Roberto reported to spring training, he and Vera were engaged. At last Roberto had something in his life besides baseball.

1964 was another very good baseball season for Roberto. He won the league batting title again with a .339 average. He also won his fourth consecutive Gold Glove and played on his fifth straight All-Star Team.

Despite Roberto's strong playing, the Pirates didn't finish anywhere near first place. This bothered Roberto. He was too much of a competitor to be satisfied with just his personal achievements. He wanted the Pirates to start winning again. Roberto wanted to win the National League's MVP Award.

But that would have to wait until another season. Roberto went home to Puerto Rico. On November 14, 1964, he married Vera in the Church of San Fernando, in Carolina.

All in all, it had been a very good year.

Roberto and Harry

When Roberto returned home to Puerto Rico from his honeymoon he planned to take it easy until it was time to report for '65 spring training. He and Vera wanted to get their new house in order. Roberto also planned to manage and play for the San Juan Senators.

For a few days everything was fine. Then, when Roberto was mowing the grass, the lawnmower hit a stone and hurled it into the air. The stone hit Roberto's right leg, hurting it badly. Roberto should have stopped playing baseball until his leg was better. But he didn't. The Winter League all-star game was the next week. Roberto didn't want to let down the people of his country by not playing.

His decision to play in the game was one that Roberto would regret.

His leg gave out during the game, and he ended up having surgery. The doctors said the operation was a success. But when spring training began in March Roberto did not join the rest of the team. The Pirates immediately announced that Roberto would have to pay a one-hundred-dollar-a-day fine until he showed up.

Vera called the Pirates' training camp in Fort Myers, Florida, to say that Roberto was in the hospital with a one-hundred-five-degree fever. He had either malaria or a typhoid infection, and the recovery period would be long. All the doctors said that Roberto had to take the entire season off.

Vera agreed with them. Roberto had lost a lot of weight, and he was very weak. She was worried that if he tried to play ball he might have a relapse. but Roberto was determined to play.

"Why don't you retire for a year, then come back? You can't play like this or you'll kill yourself," Vera said to her husband.

"No," Roberto said. "I'll go and try it."

When Roberto finally joined the Pirates he found out that Danny Murtaugh had retired because of a heart problem. The new manager was a man named Harry Walker.

Harry Walker was an easygoing Southerner

who loved to talk about baseball. Walker knew a lot about hitting. He had once won the National League batting title with a .361 average.

Harry immediately made two suggestions to Roberto. First he told Roberto to go back to a lighter bat. He felt that Roberto's swing was too slow; a lighter bat would speed it up. Second, he wanted Roberto to try to pull the ball more. Walker thought this would give Roberto more power.

Roberto tried what Walker suggested, but it didn't help the Pirates much. They lost twenty-four of their first thirty-three games. Roberto was still weak from his illness, and he was struggling at the plate and in the field.

Walker tried to give Roberto some rest by keeping him on the bench during a Pirates road trip. But then something happened that made Roberto furious. In a radio interview during the road trip Walker said, "Superstars like Stan Musial and Ted Williams played with injuries."

The manager's statement implied that Roberto was not a superstar, since he was *not* playing because of injuries. Roberto became enraged. He was convinced that Walker had set him up so that he would look bad.

65

"I want to be traded. . . . I cannot play for this man," Roberto said.

But instead of getting into a war with Roberto, Walker invited him to have breakfast so they could work out their disagreement.

"It was all a misunderstanding," Walker told some reporters later. "We tried to start him too soon after the malaria and then rest him. It was the wrong thing to do." ₍

After that Walker and Clemente got on just fine. Walker's relaxed approach to managing worked with Roberto and the rest of the Pirates. The team played well during the second half of the season. Roberto got on base in thirty-three out of thirty-four games.

The Pirates ended the 1965 season in third place. It was their best finish since they had won the World Series five years before.

Roberto finished with the highest batting average in either league, .329, and his third batting title. He had missed only three games all season.

Any other player would have been overjoyed with Roberto's statistics. Not Roberto. "I had a terrible year," he told anyone who asked.

"I was sick most of the time, and I had to push myself all year."

Harry Walker knew that Roberto hadn't had a terrible year. And he had big plans for him. "I knew the one thing in life he wanted was to be MVP. I told him some things . . . that he was our leader now . . . that he should set the example . . . that if he did, he would win the MVP award."

Walker also told Roberto to change his batting style again. He wanted Roberto to stop hitting line drives and start trying to hit home runs. Walker wanted Roberto to become a power hitter.

Roberto had always been a line drive hitter. Forbes Field's big outfield and high right field fence made it hard for a right-handed hitter like Roberto to make home runs. But Walker had faith in Roberto.

"I want you to get twenty-five home runs and drive in 115," Walker told Roberto at the beginning of the 1966 season.

Roberto had followed Walker's advice the previous season and it had worked. Roberto agreed to give it a try.

Roberto liked Harry Walker. Harry's constant talking and analyzing drove most of the other Pirates crazy, but Roberto enjoyed the chatter. He spent a lot of time listening to Harry's theories about baseball. Roberto thought that most of what the manager said made good sense.

More important, Roberto knew that Harry Walker believed in him.

The Pirates' general manager, Joe Brown, later commented on the friendship between Roberto Clemente and Harry Walker.

"The turning point in Roberto's career was Walker. Some people Harry didn't reach, but Roberto he did. He convinced Roberto he could become one of the great players of all time."

Roberto was older and wiser now. He was thirty-one years old, and he had already played ten seasons of Major League baseball. Perhaps that was part of the reason Roberto was willing to follow Walker's suggestions.

Another big change had occurred in Roberto's life. He and Vera had become parents. Their first son, Roberto, Jr., was born in 1965. Roberto insisted that Vera return to Puerto Rico from Pittsburgh for the baby's birth. He was proud to be a Puerto Rican, and he wanted all his children to be born in his and Vera's native country.

The Clementes lived in Pittsburgh during the baseball season. And in Puerto Rico they now had a magnificent new house high on a hill in Rio Piedras, near San Juan. Roberto's personal life was happily settled. He was ready to focus completely on baseball.

At first Roberto had very little success hitting home runs. By the end of May he had hit only three balls over the fence. Then he thought of something that would help him hit the ball farther.

He had always complained about the batter's box at Forbes. The area around home plate was filled with a loose, sandy topsoil that Roberto hated. He said he couldn't dig in and get the traction he needed to hit the ball.

Harry Walker was willing to try anything. He had all the sandy soil taken out and replaced with a thick, heavy clay.

It worked!

Roberto hit six home runs in eleven days. And the Pirates took off. They stayed in a three-way race for the pennant with the San Francisco Giants and the Los Angeles Dodgers. For the rest of the season, the close race excited both the fans and the players.

Something else happened during the 1966 season. It was called "the Return of the Green Weenie."

The original Green Weenie had first appeared in 1960. One of the Pirates' trainers had started bringing a huge, inflatable green hot dog to games. He would sit in the dugout and point the "Green Weenie" at opposing pitchers to "jinx" them.

In 1966 some enterprising person started making and selling new Green Weenies to Pirates fans. Whenever a pitcher from another team took the mound he saw thousands of Green Weenies waving at him.

While the fans tried to jinx the pitchers, Roberto displayed his own magic. He hit better than ever before. In September he smashed a three-run homer that was hit number 2,000 of his career. Only eight other active players had made as many hits.

Roberto even went beyond the goals Harry

Walker had set at the beginning of the season. He finished with twenty-nine home runs and 119 RBIs.

Still, the Pirates didn't win the pennant. They faltered in the last two weeks of the season, finishing third.

Roberto's statistics were mind-boggling. He had hit .317, breaking .300 for the seventh year in a row. He had won the Gold Glove for the sixth year in a row. And, of course, he'd been voted to the National League All-Star Team once again.

Most important, Roberto had become a team leader. That season he had worked with a young ball player from the Dominican Republic named Matty Alou. Alou was too small to hit a lot of home runs. But he was a natural singles hitter.

Walker asked Roberto to work with Alou. Roberto spent hours and hours with Alou in batting practice. Roberto would stand behind third base and yell, "Hit it to me! Hit it to me!" every time Alou swung at a pitch. Roberto's coaching worked. Alou soon forgot about trying for homers and began hitting hard line drives to left field.

Roberto had become looser and easier to be with. Other players on the Pirates saw the change in him. After ten seasons with Roberto, second baseman Bill Mazeroski suddenly saw a big change in his teammate. "Since Walker's been here, he's been different. He talks a lot more, hollers it up . . . It seems like he wants to win more now. Maybe that's not right to say. But it shows more."

Everything was finally falling in place for Roberto. His only competition for the National League's Most Valuable Player of 1966 was Los Angeles Dodgers pitcher Sandy Koufax. Koufax had dominated the league, winning twenty-seven games and striking out 317 batters.

But when it came time for the sportswriters to choose the MVP, they chose Roberto Clemente.

"He won the MVP because he did so many little things," Harry Walker said. "He did the things so many stars don't: hustling on routine ground balls, breaking up double plays, taking the extra base."

As always, Roberto was too honest and open to pretend that winning the MVP award wasn't important to him. As far as he was concerned, the award was six years overdue. "It is the highest honor a player can hope for," he said, "but I was expecting it.

"If I had not won the MVP, I would not have been mad because Sandy Koufax was a great pitcher and he deserved it. Besides, I know I would have been close and not been snubbed like I was in 1960."

Receiving the MVP award had an extra-special meaning for Roberto. Now kids in Puerto Rico and Puerto Rican kids living in the United States had a sports hero of their own. Roberto remembered growing up and feeling that only the white baseball players counted. There had been no one Roberto could look up to and say, "Someday, that could be me."

After he received the award, Roberto said, "I show kids what baseball has done for me, and maybe they will work harder and try harder and be better men."

Roberto had a dream for the youngsters of Puerto Rico. He wanted to build a Ciudad Deportiva—a Sports City—where any boy or girl could learn how to play baseball, basketball, tennis, or any other sport he or she wanted. Everything would be free. Poor kids wouldn't have to learn to play baseball with crushed tin cans and broomsticks, as Roberto had.

Years later Vera told a writer that Roberto was always very proud to be a Puerto Rican. Every time he won a trophy or an award, he was proud not for himself, but for Puerto Rico. "Everything he won—the three thousand hits, the batting championships, the Gold Gloves—he thought first about the island."

After winning the MVP award, Roberto signed a new contract with the team. He became the first Pirate and also the first Latin player to make $100,000 a year.

Roberto went home to Puerto Rico to relax. But it would not be a restful winter.

His brother Osvaldo finally died from his long battle with cancer. Then another one of his brothers, Vincente, died. Instead of resting, Roberto had to try and hold his family together. His parents and family needed him.

Suddenly, his great baseball season and the MVP Award did not seem so important.

A Leader for the Pirates

It was hard for Roberto to leave his grieving family in Puerto Rico and go back to playing baseball. But he did. Even though his personal life was troubled, Roberto's playing did not suffer. If anything, his performance was even stronger than it had been the year before.

The 1967 Pittsburgh Pirates had a lot of problems, however. Most of the players on the team didn't like Harry Walker. They felt he "over-coached" them, giving them so much advice that it actually hurt their playing. Some of the players just thought Walker talked too much.

Roberto liked Walker and stuck up for him whenever he could. He felt the players weren't giving the manager a fair chance. Roberto was also bothered by something else. He had found out that some players were talking about him

76

behind his back. They thought Roberto was too friendly with Walker.

In early June Roberto called a meeting of all the players in order to defend Walker and try to motivate his teammates. This was a big change for Roberto. In the old days, when Danny Murtaugh was their manager, Roberto would have kept to himself. Now, instead of getting angry, he got involved. He worked hard to keep the team strong and optimistic.

Roberto confronted the whole team. "If you have any gripes about the manager, about me, or about anything else, speak up. We can settle it here. We owe something to the fans who come to the ballpark. We have only ourselves to blame; we must stop blaming others."

The front office also had concerns about Harry Walker. He was fired in mid-July, and Danny Murtaugh came out of retirement to manage the Pirates for the rest of the season.

Murtaugh and Roberto had never gotten along very well. What would it be like to have him as manager again?

Before his first game back, Murtaugh called a meeting with the entire team. When the meeting was over he and Roberto went into Murtaugh's office to talk in private.

Whatever differences they had must have been settled in the meeting. Murtaugh and Roberto did not have any feuds or fights for the rest of the 1967 season.

Murtaugh still was not able to pull the Pirates out of their slump, however. The Pirates under Murtaugh were no better than they had been under Walker. They finished the season in sixth place.

Roberto went back to Puerto Rico determined to have a restful and relaxing off-season that winter. But his idea of relaxation was to stay as busy as possible! He played with his two sons, Roberto, Jr., and Luis. He visited old friends, played baseball in the Winter League, and made ceramics and driftwood sculptures. He also taught himself to play the organ and did odd jobs around the house.

One day Roberto decided to repair one of the two patios that were set into the hillside behind his house. As he was climbing from the lower to the upper patio, the iron bar he was holding on to pulled out of the wall. Roberto tumbled seventy-five feet down the steep hill! Luckily he didn't break any bones, but Roberto tore the muscle in his right shoulder. For the rest of the winter he had to wear a back brace.

While Roberto was recovering, Danny Murtaugh retired again. Now the Pirates had a new manager, Larry Shepard.

Shepard had spent eighteen years coaching and managing in the Minor Leagues. The 1968 Pirates were his big chance to prove he could manage a Major League team. He was determined to turn the Pirates into a top-ranking team. And Roberto Clemente was the key player in Shepard's plans.

Roberto's statistics were outstanding. He hadn't batted less than .312 the previous eight years. Winning the Gold Glove and being elected to the All-Star Team were automatic for him.

But 1968 would be a problem year for Roberto. He did not tell the Pirates about his accident until he reported for spring training. Everyone saw immediately that his shoulder was in bad shape. Roberto could barely swing a bat. All season he had a hard time making good hits, and he finished with only a .291 average.

For the first time in eight years he was not elected to the All-Star Team.

When Roberto went home to Puerto Rico that fall he thought it might be time for him to retire. If he couldn't play his best, he didn't want to play at all. But when he talked it over with Vera, she convinced him to play one more season before deciding.

Roberto rested all winter, but his shoulder still hurt when he reported to training camp in the spring. Again he struggled at the plate. At a game early in the season Roberto was even booed by the Pittsburgh fans. It was a disappointing beginning to the season, but Roberto knew there was plenty of time for him to get back into shape.

During a road trip to San Diego in May, however, Roberto almost ran out of time for good. He was kidnapped! Roberto was walking near his hotel one night when four men forced him into a car and drove him up into the hills outside the city. One of the men had a gun.

The men had not kidnapped Roberto because he was a famous baseball player. In fact, Roberto quickly realized that they did not even know who he was. They had taken him because they wanted to rob him. When the men stopped the car they took Roberto's 1961 All-Star ring, his wallet, and his clothes.

"That's when I figured they were going to shoot me and throw me in the woods," Roberto explained later. "They already had the pistol in my mouth."

Roberto pleaded for his life with the men. He finally convinced them that not only was he a ball player, he was the famous Roberto Clemente. The men must have been impressed, because an amazing thing happened. The men gave Roberto back his clothes, his money, and his All-Star ring. Then they drove him back to his hotel unharmed!

After this strange and frightening incident, Roberto's luck changed for the better. He was suddenly making good, strong hits. In the next month he pushed his average up nearly a hundred points.

Meanwhile, Larry Shepard had decided that Roberto no longer fit into his plans for the Pirates. Shepard asked general manager Joe Brown to trade Roberto for some young pitchers. Brown, who had known Roberto his entire career, refused. Instead he gave Shepard an ultimatum: If the Pirates didn't win the National League pennant, Shepard would have to find a new job.

There were many fine players on the team that year, but they weren't all playing their best. Among the promising young players the Pirates acquired in 1969 was a new catcher from Panama, Manny Sanguillan.

Sanguillan had plenty of ability, but he had started the season with a streak of errors and bad plays. Everyone could see that the young catcher's confidence was quickly disappearing.

During a mid-season Pirate slump, Roberto heard that Larry Shepard was blaming Sanguillan for some of the club's problems. From that moment on, Roberto made Manny Sanguillan into a personal project. He remembered how hard it had been for him during his first year in the Major Leagues. No one had taken the time to show him the ropes. With Roberto's help, perhaps Sanguillan would have an easier rookie year.

Roberto taught Sanguillan everything he knew: how to act in public, what to wear, how to get along with the other players, even how to get along with umpires and reporters! He also taught Manny the most important lesson a nervous rookie can learn: nobody blames a player when he blows a play or game. It's part of baseball. Once Manny realized that, it would be easier for him to stop worrying and concentrate on playing well.

Once again Roberto was showing himself to be a natural leader. And in spite of his injured shoulder, he proved again that he was an exceptional player.

Roberto had worked his damaged shoulder back into shape. Just a few months after being booed for his poor batting, Roberto nearly won another National League batting title. The outcome wasn't decided until the last day of the season. Pete Rose of the Cincinnati Reds just edged out Roberto, .348 to .345.

When the season ended the Pirates were in third place. Joe Brown fired Larry Shepard. Danny Murtaugh came back to manage the team for the third time.

Roberto did not know what the future would hold for him or his team. But one thing was for sure—Roberto was no longer the angry, young upstart who had trouble getting along with his managers and teammates. He had become a team leader. By helping his teammates, he proved himself to be a ball player who cared about much more than his own glory. If anybody could unify the Pirates and bring them to victory, it was Roberto Clemente.

A True Superstar

On July 24, 1970, over 43,000 fans packed into Three Rivers Stadium, the new home of the Pittsburgh Pirates. They came to celebrate a very special event: Roberto Clemente Night.

In June the Pirates had played their last game at Forbes Field. Walking off the field for the last time had been tough for Roberto. He had played there for fifteen seasons. It had been like a second home to him.

The crowd roared when Roberto walked onto the field at Three Rivers Stadium that July evening. As he looked around, Roberto saw many familiar faces: his Pirates teammates; his parents, Melchor and Luisa; Vera and his three sons, Roberto, Jr., Luis, and Enrique. The Pirates' ex-manager, Harry "The Hat" Walker was also there, as manager for the visiting Houston Astros.

Roberto saw Roberto Marin, the man who discovered him so many years before when he was hitting tin cans with a broomstick. Marin was still Roberto Clemente's closest baseball friend. In the right field stands Roberto could see hundreds of Puerto Ricans wearing *pavas*, the straw-brimmed hats that the workers wore in the sugar cane fields. Many of them had come to Pittsburgh from Puerto Rico just to attend this game. Everyone was there for the same reason—to honor Roberto.

To begin Roberto Clemente Night, all the Latin players on the Pirates lined up in front of Roberto. One by one they approached him, placed a hand on his shoulder, and gave him the *abrazo,* a ceremonial embrace. Roberto was very touched by their gesture. He blinked his eyes, fighting back the tears.

Then all the awards and gifts were presented to Roberto. Among other things, he was given a scroll signed by over 300,000 people in Puerto Rico. Roberto was also told that thousands of dollars had been collected and donated in his name to his favorite charity, the Pittsburgh Children's Hospital.

The entire ceremony was broadcast on radio and television to Puerto Rico. When it was time for Roberto to address all the people in Three Rivers Stadium and the fans who were listening and watching at home, he spoke first in Spanish.

"I want to dedicate this triumph to all the mothers in Puerto Rico. I haven't the words to express my gratitude. I only ask those who are watching this program to be close to their parents, to ask for their blessing and embrace."

It is a baseball tradition to play the national anthem of the United States, "The Star Spangled Banner," before the start of each game. Before the game began on Roberto's special night, "La Borinquena," the national anthem of Puerto Rico, was also played.

Then Roberto ran out to right field. He had played with the Pirates for fifteen seasons, which had included a World Series and nine All-Star Games. He had been awarded the Most Valuable Player title, four batting titles, and ten consecutive Gold Gloves. But Roberto had never felt prouder than at that moment. He did not let his fans down that night. He made two base hits and two fantastic diving catches.

Roberto played until the ninth inning.

Then, with Pittsburgh well ahead and the Astros down to their last out, he was taken out. As Roberto trotted to the dugout, the entire stadium stood, cheering and screaming their thanks.

After the game Roberto told the press what had been going through his mind during the ceremony.

"In a moment like this you can see a lot of years in a few minutes. . . . I don't know if I cried, but I'm not ashamed to cry. We are a sentimental people. I don't have the words to say how I feel when I step onto that field and know that so many are behind me, and know that I represent my island and Latin America."

When the 1970 season ended some reporters speculated that Roberto might retire. He was now thirty-six years old—ancient by baseball standards. Could Roberto still play outstanding baseball?

"Let me see," Roberto said with a grin. "I hit .345 last year and .352 this year. No, I don't think I can quit now."

Roberto was right. 1971 was not the year to quit the Pittsburgh Pirates. On his third try as the Pirates' manager, Danny Murtaugh assembled a team that dominated the National League.

Pitcher Dock Ellis was overpowering. Steve Blass, another pitcher, was nearly as good. Willie Stargell, who played left field, broke the Major League record for homers in the month of April. Manny Sanguillan was steady behind the plate and dangerous at bat.

Roberto was still complaining about assorted aches and pains, but he was playing great baseball. During a game in Houston he made a play that was dubbed "a catch for the ages" by a local sportswriter. Roberto had run at full speed to get to the ball, snaring a line drive just as it was going over the wall. Roberto's momentum smashed him into the concrete wall—but he held on to the ball.

Roberto was also having fun on the team—something that had not always come easily for him. Now in the locker room Roberto no longer kept to himself. He wasn't as loud or crazy as some of his teammates, but he was willing to take part in the practical jokes and pranks that went on in the locker room. All the joking helped keep the team loose and optimistic.

Roberto was always ready with advice or encouragement for teammates who needed it too. Once, after relief pitcher Mudcat Grant gave up a ninth-inning grand-slam home run that lost a game, Roberto stayed in the locker room after the other Pirates had left and consoled Grant.

"You helped this ball club last year and you will again. I know that you can still pitch," Roberto told the pitcher.

All season the Pirates never let up. After winning the National League East title, they met the Giants in the playoffs and finished the season as the National League champions. For the first time since 1960, they had won the pennant and were going to the World Series.

The Pirates faced the Baltimore Orioles in the 1971 World Series. The year before, the Orioles had won the Series four games to one over Cincinnati. They had four twenty-game winners on their pitching staff and one of the craftiest managers in baseball, Earl Weaver.

Most people were convinced that the Orioles would beat the Pirates. And at first it looked as if the Pirates would not win even a single game.

The first two games were played in Baltimore. Roberto played well, hitting a single and a double in each game. But the Orioles won both games, 5–3 and 11–3.

Only five teams had ever won the Series after losing the first two games. But Danny Murtaugh predicted a Pirate comeback. "Don't worry," Murtaugh said. "You haven't seen the real Pirates yet."

The Series moved to Pittsburgh for game three. Pirates pitcher Steve Blass limited the Orioles to one run, while the Pirates scored five times.

In the fourth game Roberto hit what looked like a home run, only to have it called foul. After waiting calmly while Murtaugh screamed at the umpires, Roberto hit the next pitch to right field for a single. The Pirates won the game 4–3, and the Series was tied at two games each.

In game five Pirate pitcher Nelson Briles pitched a 4–0 shutout, pushing the Pirates ahead, three games to two. If the Pirates won the next game they would be the World Series champs!

The Pirates returned to Baltimore for game six, hoping to wrap up the Series. Roberto did all he could, hitting a triple and a home run. But the Pirates lost 3–2. Now the Series was even again, three games apiece.

Before game seven Howie Haak visited the Pittsburgh locker room. Haak was the scout who had talked Roberto out of quitting the Montreal Royals way back in 1954. Roberto called Haak aside and told him that he had decided he would retire if the Pirates won that day.

For the big game Murtaugh decided to put pitcher Steve Blass on the mound. The Orioles' pitcher was Mike Cuellar. Neither pitcher gave up a hit for three innings. In the fourth inning Roberto hit Cuellar's first pitch over the left field wall to give the Pirates a 1–0 lead. They added another run in the top of the eighth. Baltimore scored a run in the eighth inning too, but that was it. Steve Blass kept the Orioles from scoring in the ninth inning. At the end of the game the Pirates had scored a 2–1 victory.

The Pirates had done it! They had won the World Series!

Pittsburgh rocked with excitement. Pirates fans poured into the streets. They honked their car horns and danced and sang. Some fans laughed because they were so happy. Others cried. The celebration was as wild and crazy as the one that had followed the Pirates' victory in the 1960 World Series.

Every baseball fan and sportswriter agreed on one thing—Roberto Clemente had been the star of the World Series. He won *SPORT* magazine's Outstanding Player Award for his performance.

Roberto had batted .414 in the Series, hitting safely in every game. He had two home runs, a triple, and two doubles. He'd also made several spectacular plays, including a throw from the outfield to home plate that had stopped the Orioles from scoring a run in game six.

When Roberto was interviewed on television after the final game in the Series, he first spoke to his parents in Spanish. "On this, the proudest day of my life, I ask your blessing."

It had been a long journey from the cane fields of Carolina. But Roberto had proven himself to be a hero.

After the 1971 World Series, Roberto changed his mind about one thing. He decided he wasn't ready to retire yet. He felt there was more that he could accomplish in baseball.

A Hero Forever

In 1972 he had another excellent season—he made his 3000th hit! But after that, Roberto Clemente never got a chance to prove how much more he could contribute to the Pittsburgh Pirates—or the game of baseball.

In December of 1972 a massive earthquake struck the Central American country of Nicaragua. In a matter of a few short seconds much of the country's capital city, Managua, was destroyed.

An estimated 7,000 people were killed. Thousands more were left without food, shelter, or water. There was not enough medicine for all the people who were injured. Nicaragua badly needed help.

Roberto knew Nicaragua and its people well. The year before he had managed a team of Puerto Rican All-Stars in a tournament there. When Roberto was asked to become the honorary chairman of the Puerto Rican Earthquake Relief Committee he immediately agreed.

Roberto threw himself into the task of raising money with the same dedication and all-out enthusiasm he had for baseball. He worked fourteen hours a day. Friends had to remind him to stop working long enough to eat his meals!

Contributions of food, money, clothing, and medicine poured in and were sent to Nicaragua. Then Roberto heard some disturbing news. Some of the supplies were being stolen in Nicaragua and resold at high prices. Many of the people who were making money from the stolen goods were the very people who were supposed to be distributing the supplies to the needy earthquake victims.

When Roberto heard what was going on he was furious. He decided to accompany the next planeload of supplies to Managua and supervise their distribution himself. No one would dare steal the supplies from Roberto Clemente.

Some supplies were already on their way to Nicaragua by boat. Roberto planned to take more supplies by plane on New Year's Eve. He would arrive in Managua just when the boat

docked. That way he could keep an eye on everything.

New Year's Day is a very special holiday in Puerto Rico. Everyone spends time with their families. For Roberto, who was on the road for weeks at a time during the baseball season, being with his family on New Year's was very important.

But helping the victims of the earthquake was even more important. Roberto was determined to go to Nicaragua.

On New Year's Eve it began to look as if Roberto would have to postpone his trip. All day there were problems and delays with the plane. First of all, it needed some last-minute repairs. Loading it took longer than Roberto had expected. Then the pilot was late getting to the airport.

"If there is one more delay, we'll leave this for tomorrow," Roberto told Vera while they waited at the airport.

Finally, at 9:22 P.M., the old DC–7 plane rumbled down the runway and took off.

Before long, there was trouble. One of the plane's engines exploded! The pilot turned the plane around and headed back toward San Juan Airport. But then there were more explosions.

The plane never made it back to the airport. It dove into the deep, dark waters off the coast.

The search for the plane and its passengers started immediately. Helicopters circled the crash site. Their searchlights swept the water for clues. The next morning the navy and coast guard brought in boats and skin divers. Pirates catcher Manny Sanguillan was an experienced diver. He came and joined the intensive search for his friend and teacher.

The seas were rough and choppy, however, and that made the work difficult. At the end of the day there was still no sign of the plane . . . or its five passengers.

Thousands of Puerto Ricans, including Vera Clemente, stood on the beach. Their eyes followed the boats, and they spoke to each other quietly. No one could believe what had happened. No one could believe Roberto was gone.

Everyone prayed for a miracle. They wanted to see Roberto suddenly walk out of the surf, alive and smiling. Once during the day the sun came out and a rainbow appeared near the spot where the plane had hit the water. That was as close to a miracle as anyone would see.

The search went on for the next eleven days. Divers found parts of the plane and the body of the pilot.

But they did not find Roberto.

After his death Roberto Clemente was honored in many ways. In Pittsburgh and in Puerto Rico flags flew at half-mast to show that the people there mourned his loss. The newly elected governor of Puerto Rico, Rafael Hernandez Colon, postponed his inauguration for four days. Streets, parks, and schools were renamed for Roberto Clemente. Newspaper editorials were written—often by the same reporters who had accused Roberto of exaggerating his injuries.

The Pirates, too, honored Roberto after his death. The team announced that they were "retiring" Roberto's number. No other Pittsburgh player would ever wear a uniform with the number 21 on it. The team also made the sad trip to Puerto Rico to attend a memorial service for Roberto in Carolina. Danny Murtaugh and

Harry Walker were both there. The Church of San Fernando, where Vera and Roberto had been married, was filled to overflowing.

People also honored Roberto by making one of his dreams come true. Money was finally raised and land donated for the Ciudad Deportiva, the Sports City for the children of Puerto Rico, that Roberto had wanted to build. Ciudad Deportiva was built in Carolina, not far from where Roberto had first played baseball.

Perhaps Roberto's greatest tribute came from the very people he had feuded with throughout his career—the baseball writers. By rule and tradition, a baseball player cannot be voted into the Baseball Hall of Fame until five years after he dies or retires.

Only a few weeks after Roberto's death, an exception was made. Ballots were printed and mailed to all the members of the Baseball Writers Association of America, the people who decide who is admitted to the Hall of Fame. On March 20, 1973, just a few months after his death, Roberto's acceptance into the Hall of Fame was officially announced. He was the first Latin American player named to the Hall of Fame.

He was inducted on August 6, 1973. One of the other players inducted that day was Monte Irvin, Roberto's first idol.

Today visitors to the Hall of Fame can see the bronze tablet that lists many of the "stats" that qualified Roberto Clemente for the Hall of Fame. But there is a lot about Roberto that is not on the plaque.

The plaque does not say that of all the players ever to wear the Pittsburgh Pirates' uniform, Roberto holds the record for number of games played, times at bat, number of hits, and total bases. It does not say that he is third among all Pirates in runs scored, RBIs, home runs, triples and doubles.

The plaque does not say that Roberto Clemente played right field with a combination of grace and power that has never been equaled. It does not say that his batting grew more powerful every year, or that Roberto still inspires young ball players everywhere.

The plaque does not say that Roberto lost his life helping people he hardly knew. It does not say that Roberto showed the people of his country, his friends, and his fans how to be proud to be black or Puerto Rican.

All of these things may not be the reasons that Roberto Walker Clemente is in the Hall of Fame.

But they are reasons why we remember him.

Highlights in the Life of
Roberto Clemente

1934   On August 18 Roberto Walker
Clemente is born in Carolina,
Puerto Rico. He is the youngest son
of Melchor and Luisa Clemente.

1948   Roberto Marin, the coach of the
Sello Rojo softball team, discovers
Roberto.

1951   Roberto plays baseball and track in
high school, and excels at both
sports. He is considered for the
Puerto Rican team in the 1952
Olympics.

1952   Roberto attends an open tryout
sponsored by the Brooklyn
Dodgers. The Dodgers are impressed with him, but Roberto is

105

too young to sign a contract. Roberto then signs a semi-pro contract with the Santurce Crabbers.

1954   Roberto signs a Major League contract with the Brooklyn Dodgers. The Dodgers send Roberto to their farm team, the Montreal Royals.

1955   Roberto is drafted by the Pittsburgh Pirates.

1960   The Pirates win the World Series. Roberto places eighth in the voting for the National League's Most Valuable Player.

1961   Roberto wins the National League batting title and the Gold Glove for the best-fielding right fielder.

1964   Roberto meets Vera Zabala in Carolina, Puerto Rico. They become engaged before spring training and marry when the season ends.

1966	Roberto wins the National League MVP Award.
1970	On July 24 Roberto is honored on Roberto Clemente Night at Three Rivers Stadium.
1971	The Pirates win the World Series. Roberto hits safely in every game and finishes the Series with a .414 batting average.
1972	On September 30 Roberto makes his three thousandth career hit. Only ten other players before him have made as many hits. On December 31 Roberto is killed in a plane crash while taking supplies to earthquake victims in Nicaragua.
1973	Roberto becomes the first Latin American player to be admitted to the Baseball Hall of Fame.